RESTING IN MY FATHER

30 Day Devotional

SHANNON SPRUILL

SMS Write On Publishing, LLC

DAY ONE: FINDING STRENGTH IN CHRIST

*A*s Christians where do we find our strength?

Life provides many challenges and sometimes hopelessness slips in, but we must remember from where we draw our strength. It is in Christ that we are made strong. We must lean and depend on Christ at all times. We must not worry or fear; be confident that we can find strength in Him. Is it easy to give into our weakness and worry about life situations? Pray and hand it over to Christ. It does not mean that your problems will disappear, but you will find comfort in knowing that Christ is going through with you and He is carrying the load. We have peace and not fear when we allow God to be our strength. The story of Gideon is an example of strength in God-Judges 6:12-16, 23 KJV: Gideon knew he was not strong enough to defeat the Midianites. God assured him that he would protect him, and he would be victorious in battle. When our strength comes from God, we can do the impossible.

Verses to meditate on:

Psalm 46:1-3 KJV -God is our refuge and strength, an ever-present help in trouble. Therefore we will not fear, though the earth give way and the mountains fall into the heart of the sea, though its waters roar and foam and the mountains quake with their surging.

Proverbs 18:10 KJV - The name of the Lord is a strong tower; the righteous run into it and are safe.

2 Corinthians 12:8-10 KJV -For this thing I besought the Lord thrice, that it might depart from me. And he said unto me, My grace is sufficient for thee: for my strength is made perfect in weakness. Most gladly therefore will I rather glory in my infirmities, that the power of Christ may rest upon me. Therefore I take pleasure in infirmities, in reproaches, in necessities, in persecutions, in distresses for Christ's sake: for when I am weak, then am I strong.

Philippians 4:13 KJV - I can do all things through Christ which strengtheneth me..

<u>Study Questions:</u>

What is your reaction when God seems to be silent when you have an urgent request?

How has God worked in and through you during a time of weakness?

What can you do to prepare yourself for those times when you feel helpless or hopeless?

JOURNAL - DATE _____

JOURNAL - DATE _____

DAY TWO: THE IMPORTANCE OF PRAYING

*W*hy is it important to pray?

In every relationship there is a communication of some sort. The same applies to your relationship with God. There needs to be some form of communication and praying is our communication with God. Praying is not the only way to communicate with God, but it is one of the most important. It is so important that Jesus provided us with a blueprint on how to pray to our Father. Matthew chapter 6, Jesus instructs the disciples on how to pray. Praying is not complicated, and you can pray anytime or anywhere. It is impossible to know someone if you don't spend time with them. There has to be some conversation in order to get to know someone. Prayer is our opportunity to get to know God. It is our opportunity to develop and deepen our relationship with God. Jesus, in the flesh, also pray to His Father often. Jesus prays in John 17 before His betrayal and crucifixion. John 11:41-42 Jesus prays before raising Lazarus. Jesus also prays at the cross - Luke 23:34, Matthew 27:46, and Luke 23:46. We are to be Christlike in all that we do, so praying is a must as Jesus himself prayed to the Father on many occasions.

Verses to meditate on:

Matthew 6:9-13 KJV - After this manner therefore pray ye: Our Father which art in heaven, Hallowed be thy name. Thy kingdom come, Thy will be done in earth, as it is in heaven. Give us this day our daily bread. And forgive us our debts, as we forgive our debtors. And lead us not into temptation, but deliver us from evil: For thine is the kingdom, and the power, and the glory, for ever. Amen.

Philippians 4:6 KJV - Be careful for nothing; but in every thing by prayer and supplication with thanksgiving let your requests be made known unto God.

Jeremiah 29:12 KJV - Then shall ye call upon me, and ye shall go and pray unto me, and I will hearken unto you.

<u>Study Questions:</u>

What is a petition?

What is intercession?

Do you believe that obedience to God's Word helps a Christian pray according to God's will?

JOURNAL - DATE _____

JOURNAL - DATE _____

3

DAY THREE: THAT GREAT COMMANDMENT - LOVE

*L*ove supersedes all in the life of a Christian.

Love is the cornerstone of the christian's life. God is love. God's love for us is undeniable. God loved us so much that he gave his only Son to die for us when we were not worthy. We were worthy of death, but God's love for us is so amazing that he spared us. Jesus, who was without sin, took on our sins and die for us that we might have access to the Father. That is powerful love; agape love, God's perfect and unconditional love. The great commandment instructs us to love the Lord our God with all of our heart, soul and mind. He also instructs us to love thy neighbor as thyself. In other words, we must strive to love like Christ. Love is an action word, so our love is shown by what we do. Our attitudes and behaviors are a reflection of God's love.

. . .

Verses to meditate on:

1 John 4:8 KJV - He that loveth not knoweth not God; for God is love.

1 John 4:19 KJV - We love him, because he first loved us.

John 3:16 KJV- For God so loved the world, that he gave his only begotten Son, that whosoever believeth in him should not perish, but have everlasting life.

Study Questions:

Describe what agape love means to you?

How do we show our love for God?

What happens to our efforts to love each other if those efforts aren't connected to Jesus' love for us?

JOURNAL - DATE _____

JOURNAL - DATE _____

4

DAY FOUR: THE IMPORTANCE OF WORSHIPPING GOD

*O*ur Gift to God!

Worship is our gift to God. Worship is our love expressed to God as a response to His grace towards us. Worship allows us into God's presence to celebrate and thank him for what He has done in our lives. During worship you feel and experience God's presence. Our worship is celebratory and thankfulness in response to the greatest gift given to us: the sacrifice of Christ that provides our salvation. That alone is enough for us to worship our Father!! There are many ways to worship God and some include; singing, dancing, reading scripture, and praying. Where do we worship as Christians? Anywhere!! We meet at church to worship God together, but you can worship God anywhere. We must worship God in spirit and truth. The Holy Spirit helps us understand God's power. The Holy Spirit moves us to worship and give thanks. The Holy Spirit leads us into the worship experience.

Verses to meditate on:

John 4:24 KJV- God is a Spirit: and they that worship him must worship him in spirit and in truth.

Hebrews 13:15 KJV- By him therefore let us offer the sacrifice of praise to God continually, that is, the fruit of our lips giving thanks to his name.

Luke 4:8 KJV- And Jesus answered and said unto him, Get thee behind me, Satan: for it is written, Thou shalt worship the Lord thy God, and him only shalt thou serve.

Study Questions:

How would you describe worship and its impact in your life?

What are some things in your life that may become a distraction and get in the way of your worship of God?

Where is your favorite place to worship God?

JOURNAL - DATE _____

JOURNAL - DATE _____

5

DAY FIVE: REPENT

*F*orgive me for I have sinned.

This should be part of your daily conversation with God. Confess your sins and ask God for forgiveness. We will never be without sin as long as we are alive and in this flesh. So we must constantly turn to God for forgiveness. Once we ask God for forgiveness, we must turn from that sin. We can't ask for forgiveness and go back to the same sin. Do we do this? Yes, but we must constantly pray and be mindful. As Christians, we grow and develop. Along with that growth and development should come change. Our walk and talk should change. Will we become sinless? Absolutely not, but we have a focus of doing right and repenting of our sins. We won't be sinless, but we will sin less.

. . .

Verses to meditate on:

Acts 3:19 KJV- Repent ye therefore, and be converted, that your sins may be blotted out, when the times of refreshing shall come from the presence of the Lord.

Matthew 4:17 KJV - From that time Jesus began to preach, and to say, Repent: for the kingdom of heaven is at hand.

Acts 2:38 KJV - Then Peter said unto them, Repent, and be baptized every one of you in the name of Jesus Christ for the remission of sins, and ye shall receive the gift of the Holy Ghost.

Study Questions:

Can we repent on our own?

What fruit in your life can you directly relate to a time when you were genuinely repentant?

Can I keep repenting for the same sin?

JOURNAL - DATE _____

JOURNAL - DATE _____

6

DAY SIX: YOUR STORY: TESTIMONY

I will testify just how good God has been to me!!

As Christians, we should all have a story to tell. That story is our testimony. What is our testimony? Is your story about how Christ has worked in your life. Your testimony should shine a light on Christ! I love the story about the lame man that Jesus told to pick up your bed and walk. I often wondered why he needed to pick up his bed. Just walking was enough to praise God! But his bed was part of his testimony. It was a reminder of where he came from before his encounter with Jesus. Now he would go and tell others about Jesus. That became his testimony. We all have some sort of testimony and we should be sharing it.

Verses to meditate on:
    Luke 8:39 KJV - "Return to your home, and declare

how much God has done for you." And he went away, proclaiming throughout the whole city how much Jesus had done for him.

Revelation 12:11 KJV - And they overcame him by the blood of the Lamb, and by the word of their testimony; and they loved not their lives unto the death.

2 Timothy 1:8-9 KJV - Be not thou therefore ashamed of the testimony of our Lord, nor of me his prisoner: but be thou partaker of the afflictions of the gospel according to the power of God; Who hath saved us, and called us with an holy calling, not according to our works, but according to his own purpose and grace, which was given us in Christ Jesus before the world began.

Study Questions:

How does testimony help others?

What does your relationship with God look like?

Is your testimony a reflection of your relationship with God?

JOURNAL - DATE _____

JOURNAL - DATE _____

7

DAY SEVEN: THE POWER OF FORGIVENESS

*F*orgiveness sets you free from the bondage of unforgivingness.

God forgives us over and over again. We see the grace of God daily in our lives. He is a loving, merciful and forgiving God. We must be obedient to the Word of God and the Word of God tell us to forgive one another even as God for Christ's sake has forgiven us. When you forgive, you are doing God's' will. Forgiveness is for your peace of mind, growth and development. When you hold on to the hurt and anger that comes from not forgiving, it disrupts your life more than the person who has offended you. When we dwell on past hurts, it keeps us from living out our best life. Extend the same forgiveness that God has extended to us.

Verses to meditate on:

Ephesians 4:32 KJV - And be ye kind one to another, tenderhearted, forgiving one another, even as God for Christ's sake hath forgiven you.

Colossians 3:13 KJV - Forbearing one another, and forgiving one another, if any man have a quarrel against any: even as Christ forgave you, so also do ye.

Matthew 18:21-22 KJV - Then Peter came up and said to him, "Lord, how often will my brother sin against me, and I forgive him? As many as seven times?" Jesus said to him, "I do not say to you seven times, but seventy times seven.

Study Questions:

What stops you from forgiving someone?

How do you feel when you forgive someone?

Why do we need to forgive someone when they know what they are doing?

JOURNAL - DATE _____

JOURNAL - DATE _____

8

DAY EIGHT: YOUR ARE NOT THE JUDGE

*J*udge one another carefully and lovingly.

Always remember that when you judge someone, you will be judged in the same way. Judging is our way of creating a pecking order of superior or inferior. And this can get us in trouble. Instead of looking to judge your brother, why not look to support and encourage them from a biblical context.

Verses to meditate on:

Matthew 7:1-5 KJV - Judge not, that ye be not judged. For with what judgment ye judge, ye shall be judged: and with what measure ye mete, it shall be measured to you again. And why beholdest thou the mote that is in thy brother's eye, but considerest not the beam that is in thine own eye? Or how wilt thou say to thy brother, Let me pull out the mote out of thine eye; and, behold, a beam is in thine own eye? Thou hypocrite, first cast out the beam out of thine own eye; and then shalt thou see clearly to cast out the mote out of thy brother's eye.

Luke 6:37 KJV - Judge not, and ye shall not be judged: condemn not, and ye shall not be condemned: forgive, and ye shall be forgiven:

<u>Study Questions:</u>

What are your intentions when you judge someone?

How can you help instead of judging?

Who am I to judge?

JOURNAL - DATE _____

JOURNAL - DATE _____

9

DAY NINE: TEMPTATION

*W*e all face some form of temptation daily.

As Christian it is our responsibility to look to Christ for help with dealing with temptation; "do not lead us into temptation, but deliver us from evil". It is also our responsibility to recognize these temptations and avoid them. You can strengthen your defenses against temptation by studying God's word, prayer, and spiritual maturity.

Verses to meditate on:
1 Corinthians 10:13 KJV - There hath no temptation taken you but such as is common to man: but God is faithful, who will not suffer you to be tempted above that ye are able; but will with the temptation also make a way to escape, that ye may be able to bear it.

Hebrews 2:18 KJV - For in that he himself hath suffered being tempted, he is able to succour them that are tempted.

James 1:14 KJV - But every man is tempted, when he is drawn away of his own lust, and enticed.

Study Questions:

What role does God play in your temptations?

What are some of the temptations that you are regularly battling?

Why do you think people try to blame God for the temptations that they face?

JOURNAL - DATE _____

JOURNAL - DATE _____

10

DAY TEN: WHAT IT MEANS TO BE CHRISTLIKE

On this Christian journey I strive to be Christlike in all that I do.

Now the question is this: If only Christ is perfect and free from sin, how can we ever truly become Christlike? Christlike means we must embody the characteristics of Christ. When we are empowered and guided by the Holy Spirit, we are able to align with God's will and take on his characteristics; Loving, Kindness, Patience and Forgiving just to name a few. We will never be perfect like Christ, but we must strive daily to take on His characteristics.

Verses to meditate on:
Romans 8:29 KJV - For whom he did foreknow, he also did predestinate to be conformed to the image of his Son, that he might be the firstborn among many brethren.

1 Corinthians 11:1 - Be ye followers of me, even as I also am of Christ.

Ephesians 4:15 KJV - But speaking the truth in love, may grow up into him in all things, which is the head, even Christ:

Galatians 5:22-23 KJV - But the fruit of the Spirit is love, joy, peace, longsuffering, gentleness, goodness, faith, Meekness, temperance: against such there is no law.

Study Questions:

How does the fruit of the Spirit relate to being Christlike?

How do I make the changes I know I need to make to become more like Christ?

Are there things I know I ought to change but don't want to change? Why?

JOURNAL - DATE _____

JOURNAL - DATE _____

11

DAY ELEVEN: THE DANGERS OF PRIDE

*P*ride causes us to think more highly of ourselves.

Pride can separate you from the body of Christ because our ego tells us we are better than....Pride replaces God. Pride makes us feel good, and it makes us feel superior based on the values of the world.

Verses to meditate on:
  Proverbs 11:2 KJV - When pride cometh, then cometh shame: but with the lowly is wisdom.
  Proverbs 16:18 KJV - Pride goeth before destruction, and an haughty spirit before a fall
  James 4:6 KJV - But he giveth more grace. Wherefore he saith, God resisteth the proud, but giveth grace unto the humble.

Study Questions:

Define Pride in your own words:

What are some of the ways pride can impact your relationships with others? With God?

Do you know when pride creeps up in your conversation?

JOURNAL - DATE _____

JOURNAL - DATE _____

12

DAY TWELVE: DON'T BE JEALOUS

*W*hat God has for you is for you and no one else.

Being jealous of someone and what they have is not a characteristic of a Christian. We do not know the journey that person had to endure to get that thing you envy. Jealousy is proof that you are giving into your desires. Jealousy sends a message that you are not satisfied with what God has provided for you.

Verses to meditate on:
James 3:16 KJV - For where envying and strife is, there is confusion and every evil work.

James 4:2-3 KJV - Ye lust, and have not: ye kill, and desire to have, and cannot obtain: ye fight and war, yet ye have not, because ye ask not. Ye ask, and receive not, because ye ask amiss, that ye may consume it upon your lusts.

James 3:14-15 KJV - But if you have bitter jealousy and selfish ambition in your hearts, do not boast and be false to the truth. This is not the wisdom that comes down from above, but is earthly, unspiritual, demonic.

<u>Study Questions:</u>

What does jealousy show me about myself?

How does insecurity contribute to our struggle with jealousy?

What can I do to release my feelings of jealousy?

JOURNAL - DATE _____

JOURNAL - DATE _____

13

DAY THIRTEEN: HEAR FROM GOD

*F*ocus on God and be still to hear his voice.

The very first thing you must do to be able to hear God's voice is to have a relationship with Him. That relationship should include daily conversations and interaction with God. Not only when you have a problem or trouble arises. Position your heart and then prepare your mind. Quiet yourself and be still. Focus on God's goodness and his love.

Verses to meditate on:
   John 10:27 KJV - My sheep hear my voice, and I know them, and they follow me:

   John 8:47 KJV - He that is of God heareth God's words: ye therefore hear them not, because ye are not of God.

Isaiah 30:21 KJV - And thine ears shall hear a word behind thee, saying, This is the way, walk ye in it, when ye turn to the right hand, and when ye turn to the left.

Study Questions:

Is there any particular time or setting where God communicates with you the most?

What are some other ways that God communicates with people?

What is your favorite example of God communicating with you?

JOURNAL - DATE _____

JOURNAL - DATE _____

14

DAY FOURTEEN: PLEASING GOD!

*L*ive your life in a way that is pleasing to God.

We must be certain that all that we are doing is to the glory of God. We must strive to please God. Will we fail at times? Yes, but repent and continue. As we anchor ourselves in His Word and continue to develop our relationship with God, it will be easier to please Him. When you are aligned with God's will, your action will be pleasing to God.

Verses to meditate on:

1 Thessalonians 2:4 KJV - But as we were allowed of God to be put in trust with the gospel, even so we speak; not as pleasing men, but God, which trieth our hearts.

Galatians 1:10 KJV - For do I now persuade men, or

God? or do I seek to please men? for if I yet pleased men, I should not be the servant of Christ.

Proverbs 16:7 KJV - When a man's ways please the Lord, he maketh even his enemies to be at peace with him.

<u>Study Questions:</u>

What pleases God the most?

What are some things you can do to please God?

How do you know what pleases God?

JOURNAL - DATE _____

JOURNAL - DATE _____

15

DAY FIFTEEN: REFLECTION

*T*oday I am reflecting on how good God has been to me.

If we take a moment to reflect on how good God has been to you, you would be in a reflective mode for a long time. First and foremost, if you are reading this, God has been good to you!!! Amen!!

Verses to meditate on:

Psalm 34:8 KJV - O taste and see that the Lord is good: blessed is the man that trusteth in him.

Romans 8:28 KJV - And we know that all things work together for good to them that love God, to them who are the called according to his purpose.

Psalm 31:19 KJV - Oh how great is thy goodness, which thou hast laid up for them that fear thee; which thou hast wrought for them that trust in thee before the sons of men!

<u>Study Questions:</u>

How has God been good to you?

What does it mean that God is good?

How should we respond to the goodness of God?

JOURNAL - DATE _____

JOURNAL - DATE _____

16

DAY SIXTEEN: YOU CAN'T SERVE TWO MASTERS

*J*esus' call to follow him requires us to abandon all other masters, because we can't serve two masters.

A master is anything that enslaves us, and that could be alcohol, drugs, lust or money. These masters are resistant to God. God says that He is a jealous God. He is a jealous God because He knows just how much we need him and we should be fully dependent on him.

Verses to meditate on:
Matthew 6:24 KJV - No man can serve two masters: for either he will hate the one, and love the other; or else he will hold to the one, and despise the other. Ye cannot serve God and mammon.
1 Corinthians 10:21 KJV - Ye cannot drink the cup

of the Lord, and the cup of devils: ye cannot be partakers of the Lord's table, and of the table of devils.

Deuteronomy 6:5 KJV - And thou shalt love the Lord thy God with all thine heart, and with all thy soul, and with all thy might.

Study Questions:

How can we ensure that we will not serve the world over God?

How much of your talk with your friends is about the Lord?

How much of your talk with your friends is about the world?

JOURNAL - DATE _____

JOURNAL - DATE _____

17

DAY SEVENTEEN: THE SPIRIT OF WISDOM

*W*isdom is the ability to discern right from wrong.

Seek wisdom from the God faithfully. Ask God for wisdom but be humble, prudent, peaceful and considerate. Study the Word of God and have a personal relationship with your Father.

Verses to meditate on:

James 1:5 KJV - If any of you lack wisdom, let him ask of God, that giveth to all men liberally, and upbraideth not; and it shall be given him.

Proverbs 1:7 KJV - The fear of the Lord is the beginning of knowledge: but fools despise wisdom and instruction.

Proverbs 19:20 **KJV** - Hear counsel, and receive instruction, that thou mayest be wise in thy latter end.

Study Questions:

How would you define "wisdom?" And how is it different than knowledge or experience?

Why is wisdom especially important when we are going through a trial?

Describe God's attitude and posture toward us when we ask him for wisdom?

JOURNAL - DATE _____

JOURNAL - DATE _____

18

DAY EIGHTEEN: CAST YOU CARES UPON HIM

*S*ubmit and surrender to God. Give all your troubles and burdens over to Him.

God cares for you and wants you to bring all to him and trust him with your whole heart. We can't hold on to our problems and say we trust God at the same time.

Verses to meditate on:
Psalm 55:22 KJV - Cast thy burden upon the Lord, and he shall sustain thee: he shall never suffer the righteous to be moved.

1 Peter 5:7 KJV - Casting all your care upon him; for he careth for you.

Philippians 4:6 KJV - Be careful for nothing; but in every thing by prayer and supplication with thanksgiving let your requests be made known unto God.

Study Questions:

Why does God want us to cast our cares on Him?

How can our faith grow when we cast all our burdens on God?

Why do we continue to carry burdens that we know God wants us to give over to him?

JOURNAL - DATE _____

JOURNAL - DATE _____

19

DAY NINETEEN: THE BODY OF CHRIST

*Y*ou who are in Christ are the body of Christ.

When Jesus was in his physical body and dwelled among us, He demonstrated the Love of God, especially through His sacrificial death on the cross. After He ascended, Christ continues His work in the world through those He has saved. The church now demonstrates the love of God, and the Church is considered the Body of Christ.

Verses to meditate on:

Romans 12:4-5 KJV - For as we have many members in one body, and all members have not the same office: So we, being many, are one body in Christ, and every one members one of another.

Ephesians 4:16 KJV - From whom the whole body

fitly joined together and compacted by that which every joint supplieth, according to the effectual working in the measure of every part, maketh increase of the body unto the edifying of itself in love.

Colossians 1:18 KJV - And he is the head of the body, the church: who is the beginning, the firstborn from the dead; that in all things he might have the preeminence.

Study Questions:

Describe some of the characteristics of a unified church?

How can you contribute to the unity of the church?

How has the church helped you?

JOURNAL - DATE _____

JOURNAL - DATE _____

20

DAY TWENTY: BECOMING WORTHY

*Y*ou are not worthy because of yourself or anything you have done. You are worthy because you have been washed in the blood of Jesus!

Although we are unworthy of God's grace and mercy, it is His love for us that allows us to be recipients of his grace and mercy.

Verses to meditate on:

Galatians 2:20 KJV - I am crucified with Christ: nevertheless I live; yet not I, but Christ liveth in me: and the life which I now live in the flesh I live by the faith of the Son of God, who loved me, and gave himself for me.

Matthew 6:26 KJV - Behold the fowls of the air: for they sow not, neither do they reap, nor gather into barns;

yet your heavenly Father feedeth them. Are ye not much better than they?

Ephesians 4:1 KJV - I therefore, the prisoner of the Lord, beseech you that ye walk worthy of the vocation wherewith ye are called,

Study Questions:

How did God demonstrate his love to us?

How shall we understand our worthiness of Jesus in view of our sinfulness?

Are you deserving of God's love?

JOURNAL - DATE _____

JOURNAL - DATE _____

21

DAY TWENTY ONE: SALVATION

*T*hank you God for the gift of your Son, Jesus Christ!

Your faith in God has allowed you to be a recipient of His grace.   Jesus is Lord and God has raised Him from the dead.

Verses to meditate on:
 Ephesians 2:8-9 KJV - For by grace are ye saved through faith; and that not of yourselves: it is the gift of God: Not of works, lest any man should boast

 Titus 3:5 KJV - Not by works of righteousness which we have done, but according to his mercy he saved us, by the washing of regeneration, and renewing of the Holy Ghost;

 John 14:6 KJV - Jesus saith unto him, I am the way,

the truth, and the life: no man cometh unto the Father, but by me.

<u>Study Questions:</u>

What is the human condition?

What does it mean for you to repent?

What does God grant in your new life in Christ?

JOURNAL - DATE _____

JOURNAL - DATE _____

22

DAY TWENTY TWO: ENCOURAGING ONE ANOTHER

*L*ift up and encourage your brothers and sisters.

As the body of Christ, it is important to lift each other up with encouragement and support. It's as simple as a prayer of encouragement or just an ear to listen.

Verses to meditate on:
   1 Thessalonians 5:11 KJV - Wherefore comfort yourselves together, and edify one another, even as also ye do.
   Ephesians 4:29 KJV - Let no corrupt communication proceed out of your mouth, but that which is good to the use of edifying, that it may minister grace unto the hearers.
   1 Peter 4:8-10 KJV - And above all things have

fervent charity among yourselves: for charity shall cover the multitude of sins. Use hospitality one to another without grudging. As every man hath received the gift, even so minister the same one to another, as good stewards of the manifold grace of God.

Study Questions:

Give some examples on how we should encourage one another?

What are some good words of encouragement?

Why is it important to lift one another up?

JOURNAL - DATE _____

JOURNAL - DATE _____

23

DAY TWENTY THREE: CIRCUMCISION OF THE HEART

A pure heart separated unto Christ!

One thing that happens during the process of sanctification is the circumcision of the heart. We surrender the things of this world as we grow in the knowledge of God. Circumcision can be painful, but the fruit it bears brings us into a closer relationship with God.

Verses to meditate on:

Deuteronomy 30:6 KJV - And the Lord thy God will circumcise thine heart, and the heart of thy seed, to love the Lord thy God with all thine heart, and with all thy soul, that thou mayest live.

Romans 2:29 KJV - But he is a Jew, which is one inwardly; and circumcision is that of the heart, in the spirit, and not in the letter; whose praise is not of men, but of God.

Deuteronomy 10:16 KJV - Circumcise therefore the foreskin of your heart, and be no more stiffnecked.

Study Questions:

What is the benefit of circumcision of the heart?

How does your life demonstrate that God has placed within you a new heart and a new spirit?

SHANNON SPRUILL

JOURNAL - DATE _____

JOURNAL - DATE _____

24

DAY TWENTY FOUR: HE IS MY PROVIDER

*T*he Lord provides all of my needs.

Jehovah Jireh - I trust Good to provide all of my needs. I will not worry because God is my provider!

Verses to meditate on:
   Philippians 4:19 KJV - But my God shall supply all your need according to his riches in glory by Christ Jesus.
   Matthew 21:22 KJV - And all things, whatsoever ye shall ask in prayer, believing, ye shall receive.
   James 1:17 KJV - Every good gift and every perfect gift is from above, and cometh down from the Father of lights, with whom is no variableness, neither shadow of turning.

<u>Study Questions:</u>

What is your greatest need today?

What are the barriers in your life that prevent you from experiencing God's presence at this very moment?

Give an example of how God provides for you?

JOURNAL - DATE _____

JOURNAL - DATE _____

25

DAY TWENTY FIVE: HE IS A HEALER

God makes me completely whole according to His will.

Jehovah Rapha - God has the power to heal you. Jesus, the Son of God came as a healer.

Verses to meditate on:
Jeremiah 17:14 KJV - Heal me, O Lord, and I shall be healed; save me, and I shall be saved: for thou art my praise.

Isaiah 41:10 KJV - Fear thou not; for I am with thee: be not dismayed; for I am thy God: I will strengthen thee; yea, I will help thee; yea, I will uphold thee with the right hand of my righteousness.

Isaiah 53:5 KJV - But he was wounded for our trans-

gressions, he was bruised for our iniquities: the chastise-
ment of our peace was upon him; and with his stripes we
are healed.

Study Questions:

Provide an example of how God has been a healer in your life?

I have prayed in faith for a healing, so why haven't I been healed?

If God is my healer, do I need to go to the doctor?

JOURNAL - DATE _____

JOURNAL - DATE _____

26

DAY TWENTY SIX : THE WORD

*L*et the Word minister to me and be my guide book to life.

The scriptures are speaking to you. These are the Words of God. God spoke, and it was written.

Verses to meditate on:

John 1:1-5 KJV - In the beginning was the Word, and the Word was with God, and the Word was God. The same was in the beginning with God. All things were made by him; and without him was not any thing made that was made. In him was life; and the life was the light of men. And the light shineth in darkness; and the darkness comprehended it not.

Hebrews 4:12 KJV - For the word of God is quick, and powerful, and sharper than any two edged sword, piercing even to the dividing asunder of soul and spirit, and of the joints and marrow, and is a discerner of the thoughts and intents of the heart.

Psalm 119:105 KJV - Thy word is a lamp unto my feet, and a light unto my path.

<u>Study Questions:</u>

Why is the Bible considered as the word of God?

What is the importance of God's Word?

JOURNAL - DATE _____

JOURNAL - DATE _____

27

DAY TWENTY SEVEN : WILL OF GOD

*N*ot my will, but the will of God!

It is so important that your thoughts and your prayers are aligned with the will of God. Do not be afraid to ask God what is His will.

Verses to meditate on:

Romans 12:2 KJV - And be not conformed to this world: but be ye transformed by the renewing of your mind, that ye may prove what is that good, and acceptable, and perfect, will of God.

1 Peter 2:15 KJV - For so is the will of God, that with well doing ye may put to silence the ignorance of foolish men:

Hebrews 13:20-21 KJV - Now the God of peace, that brought again from the dead our Lord Jesus, that great shepherd of the sheep, through the blood of the ever-lasting covenant, Make you perfect in every good work to do his will, working in you that which is wellpleasing in his sight, through Jesus Christ; to whom be glory for ever and ever. Amen.

Study Questions:

Now consider a time when you sought direction from God on a specific decision in an area of your life? How might you have made that decision differently if you focused on God and not on situation?

Does God use other people to tell me his will?

How do I know that what my heart desires is God's will?

JOURNAL - DATE _____

JOURNAL - DATE _____

28

DAY TWENTY EIGHT: HUMILITY

*H*umility is the characteristic that helps us think of others instead of ourselves.

Being humbles allows you to learn from others and not put yourself above others.

Verses to meditate on:

Proverbs 22:4 KJV - By humility and the fear of the Lord are riches, and honour, and life.

James 4:6 KJV - But he giveth more grace. Wherefore he saith, God resisteth the proud, but giveth grace unto the humble.

Isaiah 66:2 KJV - For all those things hath mine hand made, and all those things have been, saith the Lord: but to this man will I look, even to him that is poor and of a contrite spirit, and trembleth at my word.

Study Questions:

Define humility in your own words:

Can you give an example of someone from the Bible who showed humility when they could have been prideful?

How can you foster humility in your life?

JOURNAL - DATE _____

JOURNAL - DATE _____

29

DAY TWENTY NINE: TRIALS AND TRIBULATIONS

*B*eing saved does not make you immune to trials and tribulations.

Have you ever wondered why God would allow us to suffer through trials and tribulations? In the Bible we are taught that God loves us and all things work together for good. So with that being said, trials and tribulations must have a divine purpose.

Verses to meditate on:
James 1:12 KJV - Blessed is the man that endureth temptation: for when he is tried, he shall receive the crown of life, which the Lord hath promised to them that love him.

1 Peter 5:10 KJV - But the God of all grace, who hath called us unto his eternal glory by Christ Jesus, after that ye have suffered a while, make you perfect, stablish, strengthen, settle you.

Philippians 4:6-7 KJV - Be careful for nothing; but in every thing by prayer and supplication with thanksgiving let your requests be made known unto God. And the peace of God, which passeth all understanding, shall keep your hearts and minds through Christ Jesus.

Study Questions:

How difficult is it to rejoice when you are going through difficulty in your life?

When we rejoice in our trials, how does this benefit you?

How do we become more like Jesus as we endure trials and suffer well?

JOURNAL - DATE _____

JOURNAL - DATE _____

30

DAY THIRTY: BORN AGAIN

To be born again is a spiritual rebirth and you are led by the Holy Spirit.

Being born again means you are now part of the royal family of God. You are saved and no longer under eternal condemnation.

Verses to meditate on:

John 3:3 KJV - Jesus answered and said unto him, Verily, verily, I say unto thee, Except a man be born again, he cannot see the kingdom of God.

2 Corinthians 5:17 KJV - Therefore if any man be in Christ, he is a new creature: old things are passed away; behold, all things are become new.

John 3:16 KJV - For God so loved the world, that he gave his only begotten Son, that whosoever believeth in him should not perish, but have everlasting life.

Study Questions:

What does it mean to be born of water and the spirit?

How can a person be born again?

If you are a believer, who can you tell this week about being born again into God's royal family?

JOURNAL - DATE _____

JOURNAL - DATE _____